JAPANESE
GODS, HEROES,
AND MYTHOLOGY

JUN 0 8 2019

BY TAMMY GAGNE

CONTENT CONSULTANT
Keiko Rushlander
Lecturer of Japanese Culture and Director of Language Lab
Duquesne University

Core Library

Cover image: Kitsune are foxes that can shape-shift.

An Imprint of Abdo Publishing
abdobooks.com

abdocorelibrary.com

Published by Abdo Publishing, a division of ABDO, PO Box 398166, Minneapolis, Minnesota 55439. Copyright © 2019 by Abdo Consulting Group, Inc. International copyrights reserved in all countries. No part of this book may be reproduced in any form without written permission from the publisher. Core Library™ is a trademark and logo of Abdo Publishing.

Printed in the United States of America, North Mankato, Minnesota
092018
012019

THIS BOOK CONTAINS
RECYCLED MATERIALS

Cover Photo: Shutterstock Images
Interior Photos: Shutterstock Images, 1, 34–35; iStockphoto, 4–5, 11, 18, 37; Top Photo Group/Newscom, 6; New York Public Library/Science Source, 12–13, 23; Red Line Editorial, 15; John S Lander/LightRocket/Getty Images, 20–21, 45; Wellcome Images/Science Source, 25; Pictures From History/Newscom, 28–29, 43; Danita Delimont Photography/Newscom, 38–39

Editor: Marie Pearson
Series Designer: Ryan Gale

Library of Congress Control Number: 2018949764

Publisher's Cataloging-in-Publication Data

Names: Gagne, Tammy, author.
Title: Japanese gods, heroes, and mythology / by Tammy Gagne.
Description: Minneapolis, Minnesota : Abdo Publishing, 2019 | Series: Gods, heroes, and mythology | Includes online resources and index.
Identifiers: ISBN 9781532117848 (lib. bdg.) | ISBN 9781532170706 (ebook)
Subjects: LCSH: Japanese mythology--Juvenile literature. | Japanese gods--Juvenile literature. | Heroes--Juvenile literature.
Classification: DDC 299.56113--dc23

CONTENTS

CHAPTER ONE

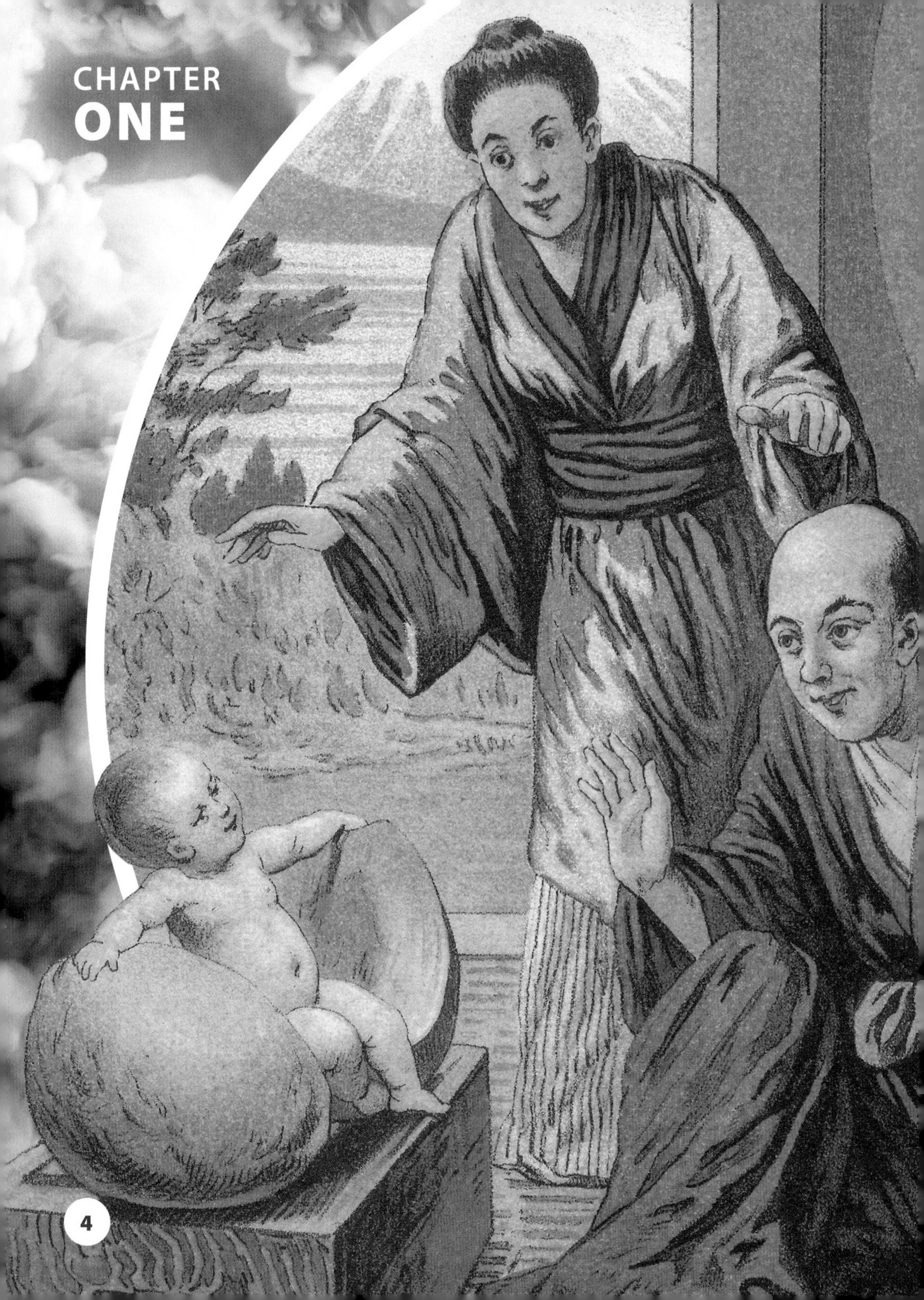

STORIES OF VALUES

Long ago in Japan, an elderly woman went to a stream to wash clothes. She saw something strange floating in the water. It was the biggest peach she had ever seen. Not having much food, she brought it home to eat. When she showed it to her husband, the peach opened up and a handsome young boy jumped out.

Having always wanted a child, the couple decided to raise the boy as their own. They named him Momotaro. He was always bigger and stronger than other boys. When he was 15, he told his father about an island filled with

The story of Momotaro, *bottom left*, is well known in Japan.

A statue of Momotaro stands in Okayama, Japan.

demons. Momotaro wanted to travel there to rescue the people from the terrible monsters.

Momotaro's parents did not want him to leave. But they knew he was meant for something great.

They gave him their blessing and food for the journey. Along the way he met up with a bird, a monkey, and a dog. He shared his food and much kindness with each of them. The animals went with him to the island. When they arrived, they defeated the demons. The people were so grateful that they rewarded Momotaro with many treasures. He gave them all to his parents so they would never go hungry again. The story teaches many lessons about the values of Japanese culture. One important lesson is the value of helping one's father and mother.

THE ORIGINS OF JAPANESE MYTHOLOGY

Most stories from Japanese mythology are found in two ancient texts. The *Kojiki* was written in 712 CE. Its name means "Records of Ancient Matters." The *Nihon shoki* was recorded eight years later. Its name means "Chronicles of Japan." The Japanese emperor Temmu ordered the creation of both texts. The stories had many different sources. Some stories had been written down in earlier books. Others had been retold by word of mouth over many years. The stories are called myths because they often involve the supernatural. Myths can reveal truths that more realistic-sounding stories cannot.

Japanese mythology is part of the Shinto religion, the traditional religion of Japan. In Shintoism, there are countless *kami,* or gods and goddesses. The kami also include spirits of nature. These spirits belong to things such as mountains and trees. Some kami were once human. They became kami after their deaths. Like humans, kami are imperfect. They can make mistakes and behave badly.

Shinto stories also explain the origins of Japan's ruling class. The myths create a family tree showing Japan's human rulers as descendants of the gods. Emperor Temmu was a member of the ruling class. He hoped the stories would strengthen his authority over the Japanese people.

During the 500s, Buddhism arrived in Japan from India. This new religion brought its own mythology to Japan. Some of the stories in the *Kojiki* and the *Nihon shoki* were Buddhist legends. Shinto is the oldest religion of Japan. But Buddhism is also commonly practiced in the country. Many Japanese people practice both Shintoism and Buddhism. Traditions of both religions are an important part of Japanese culture.

EVIL KAMI

Not all kami are good. Magatsuhi-no-kami are evil gods that bring *tsumi* to the world. *Tsumi* means "sin." It includes bad choices people make, such as murder. It also includes things beyond human control. Magatsuhi-no-kami can bring tsumi in the form of disaster or disease.

SHINTOISM TODAY

All over Japan, there are shrines built to honor the kami. A shrine is a place of worship for Shintoists. The followers believe kami reside at shrines. Followers visit to connect with these spirits. Many shrines are temples.

BENZAITEN

Some myths explain how land forms were created. One Buddhist myth tells of a five-headed sea dragon that terrified the people of Fujisawa village. Benzaiten, the goddess of music and love, wanted to help. As she descended from the heavens, an island rose out of the sea to meet her feet. It became the island of Enoshima. The dragon fell in love with the goddess. He wanted to marry her. Benzaiten refused. She scolded him for frightening the villagers. Ashamed, the creature changed himself into a hill so he would no longer scare the people. In his final moments, he turned to face Enoshima so he could look toward Benzaiten for the rest of eternity. The hill is now called Dragon's-Mouth Hill.

But natural landmarks such as mountains can also be shrines. Shrines can be large or small. Some are dedicated to more than one kami.

Many shrines have a gate called a *torii* decorated with ropes called *shimenawa* at their entrance. Some shrines have more than one torii. These gates are often made of wood and painted black and orange. Troughs of water are placed near the entrance. Visitors purify themselves by washing

SHINTO SHRINES

Torii

Komainu

Komainu, or lion-dogs, are well-known creatures from Japanese mythology. Many Shinto shrines have a pair of komainu statues guarding the entrance. It is tradition for one animal's mouth to be open and the other's mouth to be closed. If you made a shrine, what might you chose to guard the entrance?

their hands and rinsing their mouths in this water before moving toward the main part of the shrine. People visit the shrines during festivals that honor the kami. They may also visit any time they wish to pray or worship.

CHAPTER TWO

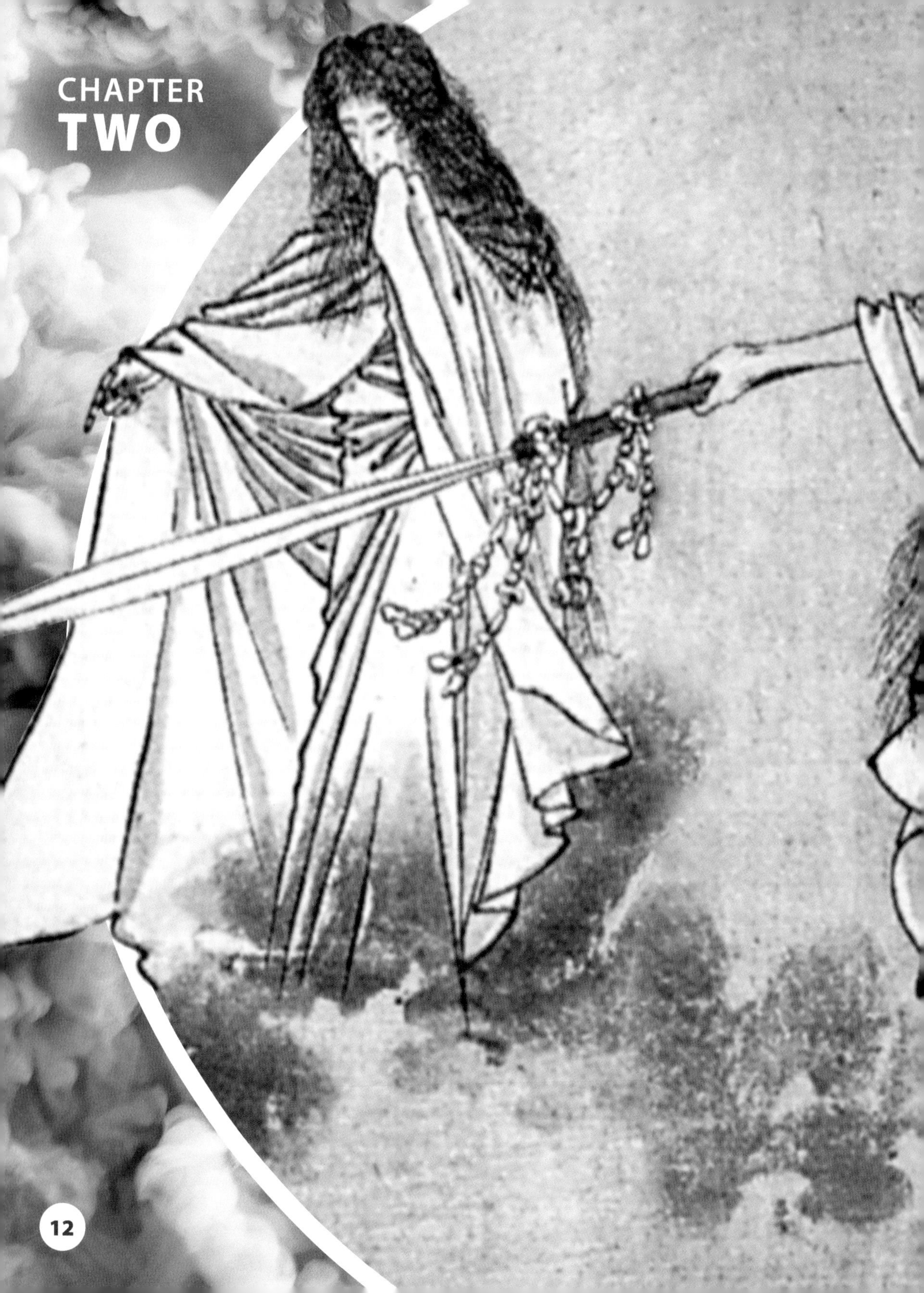

KAMI AND THE BUDDHA

Japanese myths tell how the world was created. Before the world was formed, there was only chaos. Heaven and Earth separated from this chaos, and several kami appeared, including Izanagi and his wife Izanami. They were given the task of creating what is now Japan. The pair stood on a floating bridge between heaven and the chaos below. The other kami gave Izanagi and Izanami a jeweled spear to begin their work. At first they did not know what to do with the tool. But when they dipped

Izanami, *left*, and Izanagi created the islands of Japan.

it into the moisture below them, an island formed. They called this island Onogoro.

Izanami made more islands. She made Awaji, Shikoku, Oki, Kyushu, Tsushima, and Honshu—all the islands of Japan. Many smaller islands followed. Izanami also gave birth to other kami. Her many children became the sea, the mountains, the wind, and more. The last to come was the kami of fire. Delivering him into the world burned Izanami so badly that she died.

AMATERASU, TSUKIYOMI, AND SUSANOO

After visiting Izanami in the afterlife, Izanagi was left to finish creating the world alone. More kami came into the world as he washed himself in the river. The last three of these kami came from his left eye, his right eye, and his nose. Amaterasu became the sun goddess. Her brother Tsukiyomi became ruler of the night. Another brother, Susanoo, was placed in charge of the sea. But he didn't want the job. Instead, he begged his father to send

ISLANDS OF
JAPAN

Many of the islands mentioned in Japanese mythology can be found on modern maps. Some, such as Onogoro, are not. How do you think life on islands influenced Japanese myths?

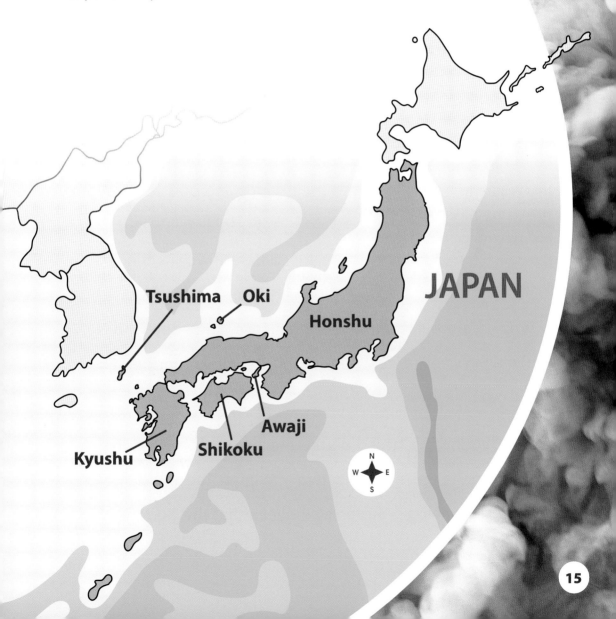

Tsushima   Oki

Honshu

JAPAN

Kyushu   Shikoku   Awaji

AMATERASU AND THE SILKWORMS

Most Shintoists see Amaterasu as the most important Japanese kami. She is associated with the craft of making silk. Japan is known for its fine silk fabrics. Although silk can now be made through other methods, many generations of Japanese families supported themselves by raising silkworms. It is said that Amaterasu could place silkworms in her mouth and pull the thread from them.

him to the afterlife. He wanted to be with his mother. Izanagi fulfilled his son's wish by banishing him to Yomi, the Japanese land of the dead. Susanoo later became the storm god.

AWAKENED

Gods and goddesses in Buddhism live in different worlds than humans. They are simply beings like humans and animals. Someone who is human in one life may be reborn as a god or goddess in the next life.

Buddhism is based on the teachings of the Buddha. The Buddha was a bodhisattva, meaning "one who seeks awakening." Buddhists believe that the Buddha lived many lives. The best-known life was as a prince named Siddhartha Gautama. He was born in India in the 500s BCE. Siddhartha's father, the king, wanted the young prince to become a great ruler. But Siddhartha did not value wealth and power. He valued kindness and peace. Shortly after taking a wife and starting a family, Siddhartha was drawn away from his palace. He set off on a journey in search of enlightenment. Enlightenment means having a greater understanding of life's truths. The lessons

THE SEVEN LUCKY GODS OF JAPAN

The seven gods of good fortune are said to ride on a Chinese treasure ship that visits Japanese harbors on each New Year's Eve. These gods are called the Shichi-fuku-jin. They include Japanese, Chinese, and Indian deities. Some are Shinto gods, and some are Buddhist. The gods bring magical gifts for the Japanese people. The items include a hat that makes a person invisible, a purse that never runs out of money, and a hammer that dispenses gold coins. The ship has a single sail with a Chinese character on it that means "fortune."

The Buddha is often portrayed sitting on a lotus flower, which is a sign of purity.

Siddhartha learned along his way have become sacred stories of the Buddhist religion.

Buddha was reborn many times. In each of his lives, he was a different bodhisattva. As Avalokiteshvara, he was the bodhisattva of compassion. He cared for people. He could give a deserving person the gift of immortality. As Manjusri, the Buddha was the bodhisattva of wisdom. This bodhisattva helped teach people. He showed them how to move on a path toward enlightenment. Buddhists worship the Buddha in all of his forms.

STRAIGHT TO THE
SOURCE

In his book *World Mythology: The Illustrated Guide*, Roy Willis describes how Shinto followers today worship the goddess Amaterasu:

> *Amaterasu is worshipped both as a spiritual divinity and as a sacred ancestor of the imperial family. She was once worshipped in the imperial palace itself, until it became politically expedient to put the authority of the emperor beyond the power of the priestesses and erect a shrine to her elsewhere. The main shrine to Amaterasu is at Ise, in Mie Prefecture. This is the most important Shinto shrine in Japan. The main building is a thatched, unpainted hut of cypress, constructed in ancient Japanese style. It is regularly rebuilt in wood in exactly the same form: from the 7th century to the 17th century it was rebuilt every twenty years; since the 17th century it has been rebuilt every twenty-one years.*

Source: Roy Willis, ed. *World Mythology: The Illustrated Guide*. New York: Oxford UP, 2006. Print. 115.

What's the Big Idea?
Read the text above carefully. What is the main idea of the passage? Name two or three details used to support the main idea.

CHAPTER THREE

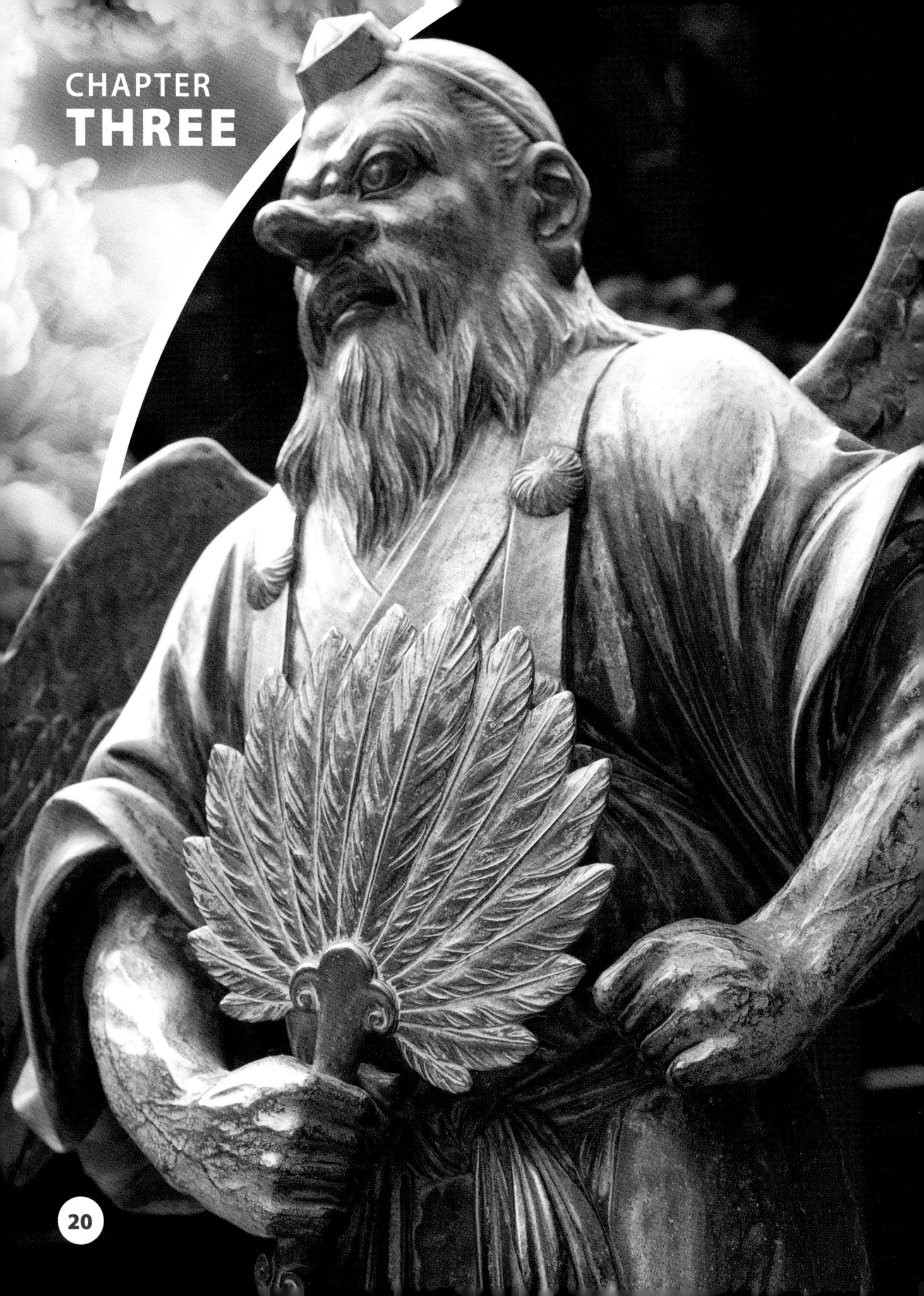

CREATURES OF JAPANESE MYTHOLOGY

Animals and other creatures appear in many Japanese myths. Their special powers often come from the animals' natural traits. This is the case with Yushkep Kamui, the Shinto spider goddess. Many Japanese women pray to her during childbirth. Like a spider, Yushkep Kamui has long legs and pincers. They help her pull newborns safely from their mothers' wombs. Myths about Yushkep Kamui come from the Ainu people.

Tengu are some of many creatures in Japanese mythology.

The Ainu people have lived on the island of Hokkaido in Japan for many centuries.

TENGU

Tengu are mysterious creatures from Japanese mythology. These mountain sprites come in different shapes and sizes. Some have human faces. Others have beaks and black feathers like those of crows. People visiting the mountains often report hearing strange voices and laughter. According to Japanese myths, tengu make these noises. They especially enjoy distracting people who come to the mountains to meditate.

KITSUNE

Kitsune are magical foxes of Japanese myths. These intelligent creatures were said to serve as messengers for many Japanese kami. Inari was one such kami. He was also quite fond of these animals. Tourists visiting Japan may notice many shrines to Inari include statues of foxes for this reason. Seeing a black, white, or nine-tailed fox is said to be good luck in Japanese culture.

Tengu are not always mean spirited. Some are helpful to humans when they want to be. Tengu have many skills, which they can transfer to humans. They are strong and skilled with swords. They can also perform magic. Tengu are more likely to help people who pay them respect.

RYŪJIN

Ryūjin is a kami who takes the form of a giant dragon. As the king of all serpents, he lives in a palace located

LIVING OBJECTS

Some Japanese myths tell tales of *tsukumogami*. Tsukumogami are everyday objects that come to life after being used by their owners for approximately 100 years. Tools, instruments, and even containers are said to develop souls after this time period. Some tsukumogami are protective of their owners and surroundings. Others may take revenge on their owners if the owners ignore them for too long.

under the sea. He also controls the tides. In some myths, Ryūjin is a great hero, while in others he is a villain. Like the sea itself, this dragon king can bring treasures or despair to those who encounter him.

In Japanese myths, snakes are seen as small dragons. Today, many people think of them as messengers of Ryūjin. Out of respect for him, many Japanese people avoid harming snakes.

MARA

One nonhuman creature in Buddhist mythology is a demon named Mara. His name means "destruction."

Artists depict the temptations Mara hurled at Siddhartha, *center*, in an attempt to keep him from becoming the Buddha.

On the night before Siddhartha became enlightened, Mara tried to stop Siddhartha from achieving enlightenment. He sent his most beautiful daughters to

Siddhartha. He hoped they would distract Siddhartha from his meditation. Mara didn't want the young prince—or any other human—to become Buddha. But Siddhartha did not lose his focus.

Mara then brought an army of monsters to claim that he, Mara, deserved the seat of enlightenment instead. He then asked who would speak for Siddhartha. Siddhartha placed his right hand gently on the ground. As he did this, the earth itself spoke up for him. Mara disappeared. As the sun rose, Siddhartha became Buddha.

STRAIGHT TO THE
SOURCE

In his *Handbook of Japanese Mythology,* author Michael Ashkenazi describes nonhuman creatures that appear in many Japanese myths. He points out that these creatures are different from creatures of other cultures in an important way:

> *Many of these creatures are "monsters" in the sense that they attack or menace humans or their doings. Nonetheless, it is useful to remember that these creatures are not "evil" in the Western sense. They are, at most, misguided, and as a consequence are suffering the penalty of this lack of law, whether the law is seen from the native Japanese viewpoint of obedience to higher authorities or through the Buddhist lens of obeying the Buddhist Law. Though occasionally it is necessary to kill such creatures, they can just as well be converted or subjugated by proper authority.*

> Source: Michael Ashkenazi. *Handbook of Japanese Mythology.* Santa Barbara, CA: ABC-CLIO, 2003. Print. 56–57.

Back It Up

The author of this passage uses evidence to support a point. Write a paragraph describing the point the author is making. Then write down two or three pieces of evidence the author uses to make the point.

CHAPTER
FOUR

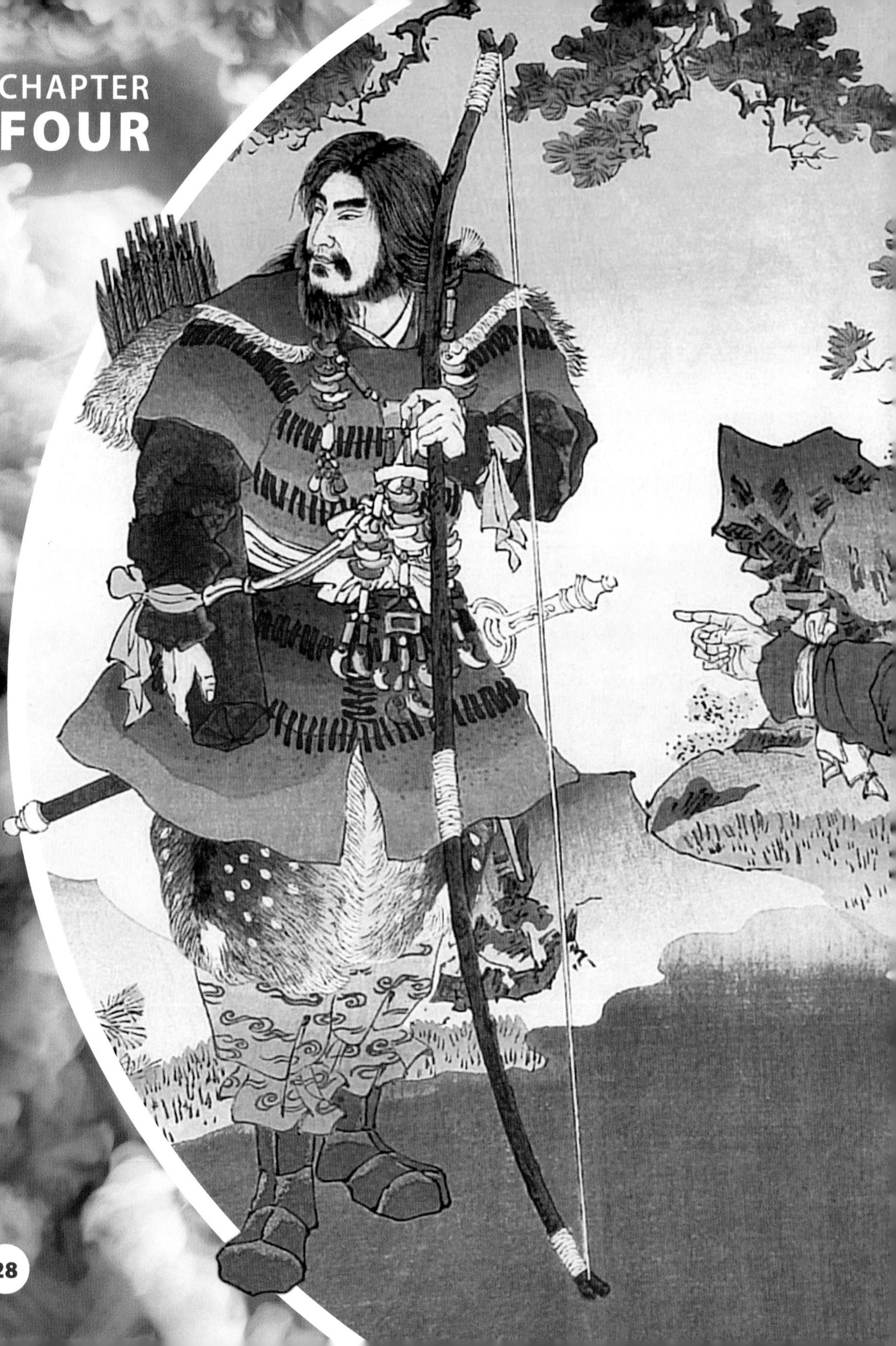

THE STORIES OF JAPANESE MYTHOLOGY

Amaterasu sent her grandson Ninigi to Earth to become the ruler of Japan. Once there, he married a beautiful woman named Konohana-sakuya Hime, or "Princess of the Blossoming Trees." Ninigi was a jealous husband. When his wife became pregnant, he accused her of being unfaithful. He was sure the child was not his. But Konohana-sakuya Hime was determined to prove him wrong. When she went into labor, she set fire to the room. She told Ninigi that the child would die if she was lying. She then

Emperor Jimmu Tenno, *left,* was said to be descended from Ninigi.

gave birth to three sons and walked through the flames with them. The new mother and all three babies lived.

This Shinto myth explains the origins of Japan's ruling family. The Yamato clan has ruled as the Imperial Household of Japan for centuries. The first emperor of Japan was Jimmu Tenno. Ninigi was said to be his great-grandfather. Jimmu is not considered one of the kami. But the Japanese people revere him greatly. The government built a shrine to him at Unebi, where he is buried, on the island of Honshu.

THE JAPANESE STORY OF DAY AND NIGHT

Several Japanese myths explain events in nature. One myth about Amaterasu explains the passing of day and night. As the sun goddess, Amaterasu brings light to the world each morning. Her brother Tsukiyomi, the moon god, takes over each night. Her other brother Susanoo, however, likes to cause trouble. Once he destroyed Amaterasu's rice fields. This made Amaterasu so angry that she hid herself in a cave.

Without the sun goddess, the world was left in darkness for many days. At last, the other gods and goddesses formed a plan. They hung a mirror in a tree outside the cave. Then, they made noises to lure Amaterasu out of her hiding place. When she came out, Amaterasu saw her reflection in the mirror. Instantly, light was restored to the world. Ever since then, day and night have passed without interruption.

TSUKIYOMI

One story tells how Amaterasu's brother, Tsukiyomi, became the god of the moon. Once, Amaterasu sent her brother to help Ukemochi-no Kami, the goddess of food. When he arrived, Ukemochi-no Kami welcomed him by offering food from her mouth. Tsukiyomi was so disgusted by this that he killed her. So Amaterasu banished him to the night sky.

SIDDHARTHA AND THE SWAN

One of the best-known Buddhist stories tells of Siddhartha as a boy. Siddhartha had a cousin named Devadatta, who enjoyed everything that Siddhartha did not. One day while hunting on the palace grounds, Devadatta shot a swan with his bow and arrow. The animal fell to the ground. Devadatta was proud of himself. But Siddhartha felt heartbroken. He rushed to help the injured animal.

Devadatta was furious. He insisted that his cousin had no right to touch the animal. He brought the matter to the royal court. He made his case by explaining that the person who shot any animal became the owner of it.

ONI

In Buddhist myths, oni are demons who cause disasters and other misfortunes in the world. They look like humans but with red, green, or blue skin. They also have horns, claws, and wild hair. Oni are also found in the underworld. They punish those who have been sent there for wrongdoing.

But Siddhartha argued that the person who wanted to help an animal, instead of killing it, should get the animal. The court agreed with Siddhartha. It let him keep the swan.

CHAPTER
FIVE

JAPANESE MYTHOLOGY TODAY

Japanese people today visit Shinto shrines and Buddhist temples for many reasons. Students often visit a shrine before an important test. Many leave notes asking the kami to help them do well. Other people may visit to ask for help with a job interview or in finding love. Large groups head to shrines on certain holidays such as Shogatsu, the Japanese New Year. Shinto priests attend events such as the opening of baseball season or the construction of a new building to bless the undertaking.

One Shinto shrine is the Heian Shrine in Kyoto, Japan.

35

THE IMPORTANCE OF PURITY

Purity plays an important part in Shintoism. Shintoists keep evil spirits away by performing rituals, or processes, to purify themselves. Every Shinto ceremony begins with cleansing. Shintoists believe that by washing their hands and faces, they are purifying both their bodies and minds. This practice comes from the story of Izanagi washing himself after visiting his dead wife in the afterlife. In Japanese culture, life and health are associated with purity and cleanliness. Pollution means sickness and death.

Shrines have become an important part of Japanese culture. Over time, the religions have mixed together in many ways. Many Japanese people recognize both Shinto and Buddhist gods. They may also practice other religions. Japanese people are very respectful of one another's religions. They rarely disrespect the beliefs of other people.

A kami can be many things. It can be elements in nature, like a waterfall. It can be the spirit of the waterfall too.

People celebrate Matsuri by playing *taiko*, traditional Japanese drums.

CELEBRATING LIFE AND NATURE

Although modern Japan is known for its advanced technology, many Japanese still value the simple things in life. Kami can reside in something as simple as a tree or a waterfall. Modern Japanese worship nature as well

as the gods and goddesses from the *Kojiki*. Visiting a Shinto shrine is a deeply peaceful experience for many followers. They consider their faith a way of life, not just their religion.

Today, Japanese myths may play a smaller role in everyday life. But they are still at the root of many special events and ceremonies. When a baby is born, parents often present the newborn to the kami at a local shine. People also celebrate kami through festivals when planting or harvesting crops. The four seasons play important roles in Japanese festivals.

Shogatsu takes place on January 1. People visit shrines to thank the kami for their good fortune in the past year. They ask for good things to happen in the next year. Rissun takes place on February 3. This holiday marks the beginning of spring. People often throw roasted beans to bring good luck and

AMATERASU, THE WOLF?

Some Japanese myths are found in surprising places today. The main character of the video game *Okami* is named Amaterasu. Although she is based on the Japanese goddess, she is different in some ways. This Amaterasu is a white wolf who must fight a mighty dragon demon to bring peace back to the world. Many other details are taken from the myth, however. In the game, Amaterasu is awoken with a magical mirror. She also uses a sword called Kusanagi, which appears in traditional Japanese myths.

cast demons away. During Aki Matsuri each fall, people show gratitude for a successful harvest.

Japanese mythology plays an important part in these celebrations. It also continues to guide many Japanese people through their daily lives. The old stories and the beliefs linked to them will likely remain part of Japanese culture for a long time.

FURTHER EVIDENCE

Chapter Five discusses how people value Japanese mythology today. Identify one of the chapter's main points. What evidence is included to support the point? Take a look at the website below. Does the information on the website support an existing piece of evidence in the chapter? Or does it present new evidence?

A GUIDE TO NEW YEAR'S TRADITIONS IN JAPAN
abdocorelibrary.com/japanese-mythology

FAST FACTS

Gods and Goddesses

- Izanagi and Izanami came into the world after heaven and Earth separated from chaos. Together, they created the islands of Japan and gave birth to many other kami.

- Amaterasu, the sun goddess, is the daughter of Izanagi and Izanami.

Creatures

- Yushkep Kamui is the Shinto spider goddess. She is known for helping women through childbirth.

- Tengu are mountain sprites who enjoy distracting humans from meditation. They can be helpful when they feel respected, though.

- Ryūjin is the dragon king who lives in a palace under the sea. He controls the ocean's tides.

Stories

- In the story of Ninigi, a jealous husband accuses his wife of being unfaithful to him. But she proves him wrong by walking through fire with her three newborn sons.

- After a fight with her brother Susanoo, Amaterasu retreats to a cave, leaving the world in darkness. But when she sees her reflection in a mirror, light is restored to the world.

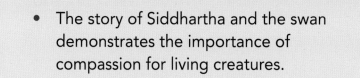

- The story of Siddhartha and the swan demonstrates the importance of compassion for living creatures.

STOP AND
THINK

Another View

This book discusses the role that mythology plays in Japanese culture. As you know, every source is different. Ask an adult to help you find another source about this topic. Write a short essay comparing and contrasting the new source's point of view with that of this book's author. What is the point of view of each author? How are they the same? How are they different?

Tell the Tale

Chapter One of this book retells the story of Momotaro. Remember, every author may tell a story differently. Using what you remember about the story, retell it in your own words to a classmate or other friend.

Dig Deeper

After reading this book, what questions do you still have about Japanese mythology? With an adult's help, find a few reliable sources that will help you answer these questions. Write a paragraph about what you learned.

Why Do I Care?

You might not be a Shintoist or Buddhist, but you may find similarities between these religions and your own beliefs. How does religion affect your daily life? What do you want to know about other world religions? Write down two or three reasons why learning about different religions is important in today's world.

GLOSSARY

chaos
a state of total confusion

culture
beliefs, art, language, and other customs shared by a group

expedient
convenient or practical

meditate
to focus one's mind for spiritual purposes

pollution
in the Shinto religion, sickness and death

purity
in the Shinto religion, the cleanliness of life and living things

shrine
a place where people go to worship

spirit
a being without a body

sprite
a fairy-like creature that, according to Japanese myth, lives in the mountains

subjugate
to bring under the control of another

supernatural
relating to things that are beyond the natural world

thatched
covered in straw or a similar material, as a building or roof

ONLINE
RESOURCES

To learn more about Japanese gods, heroes, and mythology, visit our free resource websites below.

Core Library
CONNECTION
FREE! COMMON CORE MULTIMEDIA RESOURCES

Visit **abdocorelibrary.com** for free Common Core resources for teachers and students, including vetted activities, multimedia, and booklinks, for deeper subject comprehension.

Booklinks
NONFICTION NETWORK
FREE! ONLINE NONFICTION RESOURCES

Visit **abdobooklinks.com** for free additional online weblinks for further learning. These links are routinely monitored and updated to provide the most current information available.

LEARN
MORE

Murray, Julie. *Japan*. Minneapolis, MN: Abdo Publishing, 2014.

Star, Fleur, ed. *What Do You Believe?* New York: DK, 2016.

INDEX

About the Author

Tammy Gagne has written dozens of books for both adults and children. Her recent titles include *Women in Engineering* and *Exploring the Southwest*. She lives in northern New England with her husband, son, and pets.